THE POWER OF PERSISTENCE

"……And he went up, and looked, and said, There is nothing. And he said, Go again seven times."

1King18:43

By
Franklin N. Abazie

The Power of Persistence

COPYRIGHT 2018 BY Franklin N Abazie
ISBN: 978-1-945-133-57-2
All right reserved. This book or any portion thereof may not be reproduced or used in any manner whatsoever without the express written permission of the publisher, except for the use of brief quotations in a book review. All Bible quotes are from King James Version and others as noted.

Published by: F N ABAZIE PUBLISHING HOUSE---
a.k.a,
Empowerment Bookstore:

That I may publish with the voice of thanksgiving and tell of all thy wondrous works. **Psalms26:7**

To order additional copies, wholesales or booking: Call the Church office (973-372-7518)
or Empowerment Bookstore Hotline 973-393-8518
Worship address:
343 Sanford Avenue Newark New Jersey 07106
Administrative Head Office address:
33 Schley Street Newark New Jersey 07112
Email:pastorfranknto@yahoo.com
Website www.fnabaziehealingministries.org
Publishing House: www.fnabaziepublishinghouse.org

This book is a production of F N Abazie Publishing House.

A publication Arms of Miracle of God Ministries 2018
First Edition

CONTENTS

THE MANDATE OF THE COMMISSION...........iv

ARMS OF THE COMMISSION............................v

INTRODUCTION..viii

CHAPTER 1

1. The Spirit of Persistence 49

CHAPTER 2

2. The Benefit of Persistence................................72

CHAPTER 3

3. Prayer of Salvation..96

CHAPTER 4

4. About the Author..105

THE MANDATE OF THE COMMISSION

"THE MOMENT IS DUE TO IMPACT YOUR WORLD THROUGH THE REVIVAL OF THE HEALING & MIRACLE MINISTRY OF JESUS CHRIST OF NAZARETH.

I AM SENDING YOU TO RESTORE HEALTH UNTO THEE AND I WILL HEAL THEE OF THY WOUNDS, SAID THE LORD OF HOST."

ARMS OF THE COMMISSION

1) F N Abazie Ministries-Miracle of God Ministries (Miracle Chapel Intl)

2) F N Abazie TV Ministries: Global Television Ministry Outreach.

3) F N Abazie Radio Ministries: Radio Broadcasting Outreach.

4) F N Abazie Publishing House: Book Publication.

5) F N Abazie Bible School: also called Word of Healing Bible School (W.O.H.B.S)

6) F N Abazie Evangelistic Ass: Miracle of God Ministries: Global Crusade

7) Empowerment Bookstore: Book distribution.

8) F N Abazie Helping Hands: Meeting the help of the needy world wide

9) F N Abazie Disaster Recovery Mission: Global Disaster Recovery.

10) F N Abazie Prison Ministry: Prison Ministry for all convicts "Second chance"

Some of our ministry arms are waiting the appointed time to commence

FAVOR CONFESSION

Father thank you for making me righteous and accepted through the blood of Jesus Christ. Because of that, I am blessed and highly favored by God. I am the subject of your affection. Your favor surrounds me as a shield, and the first thing that people see around me is your favored shield.

Thank you that I have favor with you and man today. All day long people go out of their way to bless me and help me. I have favor with everyone that I deal with today. Doors that were once closed are now opened for me. I receive preferential treatment, and I have special privileges, I am Gods favored child.

No good thing will he withhold from me. Because of Gods favor my enemies cannot triumph over my life. I have supernatural increase and promotion. I declare restoration to everything that the devil has stolen from my life. I have honor in the midst of my adversaries and an increase in assets, especially in real estate and expansion of

Because I am highly favored by God, I experience great victories, supernatural turnarounds, and miraculous breakthrough in the midst of great impossibilities. I receive recognition, prominence, and honor. Petitions are granted to me even by ungodly authorities. Policies, rules, regulations, and laws are changed and reverse on my behalf.

I win battles that I don't even have to fight, because God fights them for me. This is the day, the set time and the designated moment for me to experience the free favor of God, that profusely and lavishly abound on my behalf in Jesus name. **Amen.**

INTRODUCTION

"And it came to pass at the seventh time, that he said, Behold, there ariseth a little cloud out of the sea, like a man's hand. And he said, Go up, say unto Ahab, Prepare thy chariot, and get thee down that the rain stop thee not."
1King18:44

I may never get the chance to meet you face to face. But I am glad you are reading this small book: *The Power of Persistence*.

This is a book of motivation, and encouragement as inspired by the Holy Spirit. It is a book, designed to encourage, and motivate everyone going through the inevitable challenges of life. Apostle Paul said the other day *"For a great door and effectual is opened unto me, and there are many adversaries."* **1cor16:9**.

For unless we resist the devil, persist on our quest to achieve our desire in life, we will never make a mark.

Jesus made it clear to us all. The fact that we are born again, speak in tongue, sanctified, and Holy Ghost filled, does not eliminate anyone of us from facing the challenges and obstacles of life.

"These things I have spoken unto you, that in me ye might have peace. In the world ye shall have tribulation: but be of good cheer; I have overcome the world." **John16:33**

Success in life, *I believe is built upon the spirit of persistence*. If you must succeed in life, you must persist, resist, and withstand all the wiles, and schemes of the devil.

The truth is, winners do not quit and quitter never win in life. I love to say that if we must succeed in life we must resist the devil but persist in our quest to prevail. If we must prevail against challenges in life, we must embrace the *spirit of persistence*.

Those who prevail in life never give up in their quest to succeed. *"For a just man falleth seven times, and riseth up again: but the wicked shall fall into mischief."* **Proverb24:16**

The Holy Spirit revealed to us that there are relevant techniques necessary for our survival, and victory in life. I believe God is talking to us all.

Therefore, come with me as the Holy Spirit ministers to us the *mysteries of the spirit of persistence*. You will succeed in Jesus Name. Amen.

Happy Reading!

HIS DESTINY WAS THE CROSS....

HIS PURPOSE WAS LOVE.....

HIS REASON WAS YOU....

"For a just man falleth seven times, and riseth up again: but the wicked shall fall into mischief."

Proverb24:16

"And said to his servant, Go up now, look toward the sea. And he went up, and looked, and said, There is nothing. And he said, Go again seven times."

1king18:43

"And it came to pass at the seventh time, that he said, Behold, there ariseth a little cloud out of the sea, like a man's hand. And he said, Go up, say unto Ahab, Prepare thy chariot, and get thee down that the rain stop thee not."

1king18:44

Persistence Prayer points

"If ye shall ask any thing in my name, I will do it." **John14:14**

Holy Spirit of God frustrate and disappoint, every one that is against my life and family, in the name of Jesus.

Father Lord destroy every demonic networks and traps against my progress in life in the name of Jesus.

Fire of God, destroy every demonic projection and curses against my life and destiny in the name of Jesus.

Every spell and curses pronounced against my destiny, break, in the name of Jesus.

Hand of God cage every power militating against my rising in life, in the name of Jesus.

Power of God silent every voice raising a counter motion against my elevation, in the mighty name of Jesus.

Blood of Jesus neutralize every spirit of Balaam hired to hinder my life, ministry, and career, the name of Jesus.

Fire of God destroy every curse that I have brought into my life through ignorance and disobedience, break by fire, in the name of Jesus.

Ancient of day destroy every power harassing my ministry in the name of Jesus.

Father God deliver me from invincible forces militating against my life and destiny.

Power of God frustrate every coven and demonic network, designed to frustrate and hinder my success in life, in the name of Jesus.

I dismantle every strong hold designed to imprison my talent in the mighty name of Jesus.

I reject every cycle of frustration, in the name of Jesus.

Power of God paralyze every agent assigned to frustrate my life in the name of Jesus.

Finger of God, grant me supernatural speed against all my contenders in the name of Jesus.

By the blood of Jesus, I destroy every familiar spirit caging my life and career.

Fire of God arrest every demonic agents, assigned to police my destiny and marriage.

By the blood of Jesus, I proclaim no weapon fashioned against me shall ever prosper.

Holy Spirit of God break me through and forward in life in the mighty name of Jesus.

God, smash me and renew my strength, in the name of Jesus.

Holy Spirit, open my eyes to see beyond the visible to the invisible, in the name of Jesus.

Father Lord grant me strength and power in the name of Jesus.

O Lord, liberate my spirit to follow the leading of the Holy Spirit.

Holy Spirit, teach me to pray through problems instead of praying about, it in the name of Jesus.

Father Lord, deliver me from the false accusation in life, in the name of Jesus.

By the blood of Jesus, every evil spiritual padlock and evil chain hindering my success, be roasted, in the name of Jesus.

By the blood of Jesus I rebuke every spirit of spiritual deafness and blindness in my life, in the name of Jesus.

Father Lord, empower me to dominate the enemy of my destiny in the name of Jesus.

Jesus Christ of Nazareth, heal my infirmities in the name of Jesus.

Lord, anoint my eyes and my ears that they may see and hear wondrous things from heaven.

Father Lord, anoint me with power and authority to dominate all my enemies in the name of Jesus.

Fire of God roast every giant rising up against my life and career.

Holy Spirit of God destroy all my oppressors in the name of Jesus.

Angels of good new, bring my good news to me in the mighty name of Jesus.

Every strong man holding me down, lose your hold now in the name of Jesus.

I nullify every demonic prediction over my life in the name of Jesus.

By the blood of Jesus, I flush out every polluted deposit of the enemy in my life.

By the blood of Jesus, I paralyze every enemy of my promotion in the name of Jesus.

Father Lord, destroy any power tormenting my life that is not from you.

Holy Ghost fire, ignite the fire of revival in my life.

By the blood of Jesus, I declare victory over every conflicting trial.

By the Blood of Jesus, I command the arrest of every demonic spirit, militating against my life.

By the blood of Jesus, I proclaimed the blood of Jesus, over every device of the enemy.

By the blood of Jesus, I revoke stagnation and hardship over my life in the name of Jesus.

Holy Ghost fire, destroy every satanic arrangement in my life, in the name of Jesus.

Circular problems, assigned to my life, you will not prosper, backfire, in the name of Jesus.

Every satanic project, against my breakthrough, explode in the face of the enemy, in the name of Jesus.

Every dream of backwardness, go back to your senders, in the name of Jesus.

Any power, working round the clock, with dark powers, against my life, perish, in the name of Jesus.

Every household Cain, assigned to waste my Abel, you will not succeed, rush to your grave and die, in the name of Jesus.

Every domestic enemy, anointed by Satan, to terminate my life, terminate your own life, in the name of Jesus.

Anti-Christ power of my father's house, assigned to punish me, die, in the name of Jesus.

Every satanic contact of my father's house, hunting for my life, die, in the name of Jesus.

Every magician, astrologer and diviner, assigned against me, go back to your senders, in the name of Jesus.

Every evil progress, against my life, perish, in the name of Jesus.

Mid-night and mid-day arrows, fired at me, collide on the Rock of Ages and backfire, in the name of Jesus.

Every giant, occupying my promised land, lose your hold, in the name of Jesus.

By the power that silenced Sennacherib, I silence my adversaries forever, in the name of Jesus.

Every wicked altar, harboring my name and my picture, collide with thunder and die, in the name of Jesus.

Every affliction, targeted at me, explode in the hands of your owners, in the name of Jesus.

Every king Saul of my household, pursuing my David, die, in the name of Jesus.

Satanic grave digger of my father's house, dig your own grave and enter into it, in the name of Jesus.

Any power that has joined witchcraft and occult group to attack me, thus said the Lord, suffer not a witch to live, lose your life for my sake, in the name of Jesus.

Arrows of shame, disgrace, and mockery, fired into my life, backfire, in the name of Jesus.

Arrows of rise and fall, fired at me, expire, in the name of Jesus.

Every vulture of darkness, assigned to eat my flesh, go back to your senders, in the name of Jesus.

Every verdict of darkness, issued against me, backfire, in the name of Jesus.

Every dominant wicked power of my father's house, I bury you now, in the name of Jesus.

Every satanic traditional manipulation, assigned to remove my glory, fail, in the name of Jesus.

Any power, assigned to make me irrelevant in my generation, your time is up, die, in the name of Jesus.

Any power, giving me a deadline to die, fall down, and die on your own deadline, in the name of Jesus.

Every strange material and strange deposit, in my body, disappear now and go back to your senders, in the name of Jesus.

Every satanic payroll, where my enemies registered my name, I delete my name and substitute it with the names of the enemies, in the name of Jesus.

Any wicked hand, collecting evil against me, decay, and die, in the name of Jesus.

By the power that silenced Haman in favor of Mordecai, O Lord, let every power assigned against my existence, die, in the name of Jesus.

Any power assigned to manipulate my destiny, enough is enough, scatter, in the name of Jesus.

Every assembly of the wicked, delegated to destroy my destiny, scatter, in the name of Jesus.

Every ancient strongman, laboring to waste my efforts, my life is not your victim, expire, in the name of Jesus.

Every wicked mouth, sowing evil seeds against me, I command the seeds to catch fire, in the name of Jesus.

Every ancient gate, standing against my breakthroughs, scatter, in the name of Jesus.

I plug my destiny, into the mystery of divine favor, in the name of Jesus.

O thou that troubled the Israel of Miracles of God Ministries, the God of Elijah shall trouble you today.

Every enemy, of the Miracles of God Ministries, scatter, in the name of Jesus.

O God, arise and uproot anything you did not plant inside the Miracles of God Ministries, in Jesus' name.

You fire of revival, fall upon Miracles of God Ministries, in the name of Jesus.

It is written, *"Do not be afraid of sudden terror; nor of the trouble from the wicked when it comes; for the Lord will be your confidence. And will keep your foot from being caught."* **(Proverb 3:26)**.

Therefore, O Lord, cover us and our loved ones from the activities of terrorists, in Jesus name!

It is written, *"Avenge me of my adversary."* **(Luke. 18:3)**.

Therefore, O Lord, arise and avenge us of all my adversaries in the name of Jesus!

It is written, *"They fought from the heavens; the stars from their courses fought against Sisera."* **(Judges. 5:20)**.

Therefore O heavens, fight for us in Jesus name!

It is written, *"I will purge the rebels from among you, and those who transgress against me; I will bring them out of the country where they dwell, but they shall not enter the land of Israel. They will know that I am the Lord."* **(Ezekiel. 20:38)**

Therefore, O Lord, purge and sanitize our household in the name of Jesus!

It is written, *"Then it was so, after all your wickedness – "woe, woe to you!" says the Lord God."* **(Ezekiel. 16:23)**

Therefore, woe unto all the vessels that the enemy is using to do us harm in the name of Jesus!

It is written, *"Behold therefore, I stretch out my hand against you, admonished your allotment, and gave you up to the will of those who hate you..."* **(Ezekiel. 16:27)**

Therefore, let our enemies be delivered into the hands of their enemies in Jesus name!

It is written, *"You shall be for fuel of fire; your blood shall be in the midst of the land. You shall not be remembered, for I the Lord have spoken."* **(Ezekiel. 21:32)**

Therefore, let all our spiritual enemies become fuel for divine fire in Jesus name!

It is written, *"Then they will know that I am the Lord, when I have set a fire in Egypt and all her helpers are destroyed."* **(Ezekiel. 30:8)**.

Therefore, O Lord, let all the helpers of our enemies be destroyed in the name of Jesus.

It is written, *"And the people to whom they prophesy shall be cast out in the streets of Jerusalem because of the famine and the sword; they will have no one to bury them – them nor their wives, their sons nor their daughters – for I will pour their wickedness on them."* **(Jer. 14:16)**.

Therefore, O Lord, pour the wickedness of those who seek to destroy us upon their own heads in the name of Jesus!

It is written, *"Call together the archers against Babylon. All you who bend the bow encamp against it all around; let none of them escape. Repay her according to her work; According to all she has done, do to her; for she has been poured against the Lord, against the Holy one of Israel."* **(Jer. 50:29)**.

Therefore, let all the hosts of the Lord turn against our spiritual enemies in Jesus name!

It is written, *"Let God arise, let His enemies be scattered; let those also who hate him flee before him."* **(Psalms. 68:1)**.

Therefore, O God, arise and let all your enemies in our lives be scattered in Jesus name!

It is written, *"And He that searches the hearts knows what the mind of the spirit is, because He makes intercession for the saints according to the will of God."* **(Romans 8:27)**

Therefore, the intercessory prayers of Jesus, who is seated on the right hand of the throne of God, will not be in vain over our lives, in the name of Jesus.

It is written, *"The Lord is your keeper; the Lord is the shade at your right hand. The sun shall not strike you by day, nor the moon by night. The Lord shall preserve you from all evil; He shall preserve your soul. The Lord shall preserve our going out and our coming in from this time forth, and even forevermore."* **(Psalms. 121:5-8)**

Therefore, O Lord, spread your covering of fire and the blood of Jesus over us and our loved ones, in the name of Jesus.

It is written, *"Rejoice always, pray without ceasing, in everything give thanks; for this is the will of God in Christ Jesus for you."* **(1 Thess. 5:16:18)**.

Therefore, we thank you Father, for raising a spiritual shield over our loved ones and us. Thank you for giving us the heart for appreciating everything you are doing for us. Thank you for filling our hearts and our home with joy and peace that surpasses all understanding. Blessed be your name for all the answers to our prayers in the name of Jesus!

You are holy, holy, Lord God Almighty, who was and is and is to come, Amen!

O Lord, let our season of divine intervention appear in the name of Jesus!

O you gates in the heavenlies standing against our destiny, lift up your heads in the name of Jesus!

O you gates in the waters standing against our destiny, lift up your heads in the name of Jesus!

O you gates in the earth standing against our destiny, lift up your heads in the name of Jesus!

O you gates under the earth standing against our destiny, lift up your heads in the name of Jesus!

O God, arise and destroy every gate keeper assigned against our lives in the name of Jesus!

We break the backbone of every spirit of scarcity in our lives in the name of Jesus!

O Lord anoint our eyes to see divine opportunities in the name of Jesus!

Lord let every blindness to the treasures of our lives be cleared in the name of Jesus!

Let our divine helpers appear in the name of Jesus!

We declare, O Lord, that the rest of our lives will be better than the first part, in Jesus name!

We declare, O Lord that will overcome obstacles and defeat every enemy, in Jesus name!

We declare, O Lord that every blessing and promise that you put in our hearts will come to pass because this is our time for favor, in Jesus name!

We declare, O Lord that this is a new season of increase in our lives. We speak health, wisdom, creativity, divine connections, and supernatural opportunities. They are coming our way, in Jesus name!

We declare, O Lord that we choose faith over fear. We are victorious in faith, in Jesus name!

We declare, O Lord that that we are not just surviving, this is our time to thrive in prosperity, in Jesus name!

We declare, O Lord that we will believe that we have received in the spirit even though we do not see anything happening in the flesh, in Jesus name!

We declare, O Lord that our rewards are being transferred to us because we remain in faith, in Jesus name!

We declare, O Lord that doubt will not ruin our optimistic spirit, in Jesus name!

We declare, O Lord that we are prisoners of hope and get up every morning expecting your favor, in Jesus name!

We declare, O Lord that you will do amazing things in our lives, in Jesus name!

We declare, O Lord that we are closer to your abundant blessing than we think, our time has come, your promises will come to pass, in Jesus name!

We declare, O Lord that we will stay in an attitude of faith and expectation, in Jesus name!

We declare, O Lord that we are not worried, we know that you are our vindicator. It may seem to be taking a long time, but we will reap in due season if trust in you Lord, in Jesus name!

We declare, O Lord that you know the secret petitions our heart and we believe that they will come to fulfilment, in Jesus name!

We declare, O Lord that you will open new doors for us, in Jesus name!

We declare, O Lord that we will see your goodness, in Jesus name!

We declare, O Lord that this is our time to believe because favor is coming our way, in Jesus name!

We declare, O Lord that you have paved the way to abundant prosperity for us, prosperity more than we can every dream of or imagine, for your sake, in Jesus name!

We declare, O Lord that in your eyes our future is extremely bright, in Jesus name!

We declare, O Lord that we will rise higher and higher and see more of your favor and blessings and we will live the prosperous life you have in store for us, in Jesus name!

We declare, O Lord that we may have a lot of troubles, but we know that everything is going to be alright, in Jesus name!

We declare, O Lord that we have faith because we have put you first, in Jesus name!

We thank you, O Lord that our set time for favor is here, in Jesus name!

We declare, O Lord that our hour of deliverance has come, in Jesus name!

We declare, O Lord that there is no limit to what we can do, in Jesus name!

We declare, O Lord that there is no obstacle we cannot overcome, in Jesus name!

We declare, O Lord that that we have seen your accomplishments and they are good, in Jesus name!

We declare, O Lord that there is no challenge that is too great for us because you are with us, in Jesus name!

We declare, O Lord that you always succeed, in Jesus name!

We declare, O Lord that there is no financial difficulty or situation in our lives that is too great for you to resolve, in Jesus name!

We declare, O Lord that you are our Father Jehovah Jireh and that you own everything and you are our provider, in Jesus name!

We declare, O Lord that your promises declare that we are destined to live a victorious life, in Jesus name!

We declare, O Lord that we are your children, in Jesus name!

We declare, O Lord that the seeds of increase, success, and promotion are taking a new root; your favor will spring forth in our lives in a great way; we will see new seasons of blessings and new seasons of your favor. It's our time to have abundant faith, in Jesus name!

O Lord, it is written, *"According to your faith, it will be done unto you."* **Ps. 2:8** says *"Ask me and I will give you the nations as your inheritance."*

Therefore, we ask you Lord to fulfil our highest hopes and dreams, in Jesus name!

We ask you this day, O Lord to give us our abundant blessing now, in Jesus name!

We dare to exercise our faith by asking you O Lord so that we may receive indeed, in Jesus name!

We thank you O Lord that for encouraging our faith, in Jesus name!

We declare, O Lord that this is our time for favor, in Jesus name!

We declare, O Lord that this is our time to prosper abundantly, in Jesus name!

We declare, O Lord that this is our time to have instant answers to prayer, in Jesus name!

We declare, O Lord that this is our time to ask and receive, in Jesus name!

We declare, O Lord that this is our time to thank you and testify for answered prayer, in Jesus name!

We declare, O Lord that we are blessed and that goodness and mercy are following us right now, in Jesus name!

We declare, O Lord that you favor is surrounding us like a shield – you prosper us even in the desert, in Jesus name!

We declare, O Lord that you have great things for us in the spirit and that you have already released favor into our prayers, in Jesus name!

We declare, O Lord that you are a great and Holy God, in Jesus name!

It is written, *"Delight yourself in the Lord and he will give you the desires of your heart."* **(Ps 37:4)**.

We therefore declare, O Lord that we delight in you because you are our Father God and because we are your children you have made us the head and not the tail. You want to take us to a new level of prosperity, in Jesus name!

We declare, O Lord that because we are your children, we are more than conquerors, in Jesus name!

We declare, O Lord that we are blessed and you supply all our needs. We have more than enough, in Jesus name!

We declare, O Lord that we have abundant favor indeed, in Jesus name!

We declare, O Lord that we are filled indeed with the presence of the Holy Spirit, in Jesus name!

We declare, O Lord that we have abundant faith indeed, in Jesus name!

We declare, O Lord that you have answered our prayers, in Jesus name!

We declare, O Lord that our debts are all paid up, in Jesus name!

We declare, O Lord that we are healthy, in Jesus name!

We declare, O Lord that we have no lack and that we have more than enough, in Jesus name!

We declare, O Lord that we are extremely blessed so much that we can bless your kingdom, in Jesus name!

We declare, O Lord that we are extremely blessed so much that we can bless others, in Jesus name!

We declare, O Lord that we have entered into an anointing of ease, in Jesus name!

We declare, O Lord that for every opportunity we have missed, every chance we've blown, you will turn the clock and bring bigger and better things across our path, in Jesus name!

We declare, O Lord that we will not settle for less than your best, in Jesus name!

Please restore the time that we have lost, O Lord that, in Jesus name!

Restore our victories, O Lord, in Jesus name!

Restore our lost joy, lost peace, lost health, lost insight, lost faith, lost dedication, and desire to please you, we declare, O Lord in Jesus name!

We declare, O Lord that you use what was meant for our harm to our advantage, in Jesus name!

We declare, O Lord that you are a faithful God, in Jesus name!

We declare, O Lord that you will blossom our lives in ways that we can never imagine, in Jesus name!

We know, O Lord that you will bless us abundantly, in Jesus name!

We know, O Lord that you will provide divine connections, in Jesus name!

We declare, O Lord that we are not suffering – we are blessed, in Jesus name!

We declare, O Lord that our difficulties will give way to new growth, new opportunities, and new vision, in Jesus name!

O Lord let us see your blessing bloom in our lives in ways we would never dreamt possible, in Jesus name!

We declare, O Lord that we will stay in faith, so that what was meant to stop us will not be a stumbling block but a stepping stone taking us to a higher level, in Jesus name!

We declare, O Lord that we are not ordinary, but we are children of the Most High God, in Jesus name!

We declare, O Lord that we created to rise above problems, in Jesus name!

We declare victory over strife O Lord, in Jesus name!

We declare, O Lord that no weapon formed against us shall prosper, in Jesus name!

We declare, O Lord that we are healthy and that no sickness shall live in us, in Jesus name!

We declare, O Lord that triumph is our birthright, in Jesus name!

We declare, O Lord that our setbacks are simply setups for greater comebacks that will place us to be better than we were before, in Jesus name!

We declare, O Lord that with you all things are possible, in Jesus name!

We declare, O Lord that we are in agreement with you. We know you have supernatural favor in store for us. You have supernatural opportunities, supernatural healing, and supernatural restoration, in Jesus name!

We declare, O Lord that you want to do unusual things in our lives, in Jesus name!

We declare, O Lord that in faith, we have expectation deep in our spirits, in Jesus name!

We declare, O Lord that this will not be a survival year but a supernatural year in which you will abundantly come through for us, in Jesus name!

We believe, O Lord that you have come through for us, in Jesus name!

We declare, O Lord that because we hope in you, we will not be put to shame, in Jesus name!

We declare, O Lord that your word is right and true, you are faithful in all you do, in Jesus name!

We declare, O Lord that you are our refuge and strength, an ever present helper, in Jesus name!

We declare, O Lord that we will cast our cares on you and you will sustain us, you will never let the righteous fall, in Jesus name!

We declare, O Lord that you are the strength of our hearts and our portion forever, in Jesus name!

We declare, O Lord that you are our dwelling, therefore, no harm will befall us, and no disaster will come near our tent, in Jesus name!

We declare, O Lord that you are our refuge and our fortress, in Jesus name!

We declare, O Lord that you will command your angels concerning us to guard us in all our ways, in Jesus name!

We declare, O Lord that even in darkness the light will dawn for us, in Jesus name!

We declare, O Lord that your word is eternal and stands firm in the heavens, in Jesus name!

We declare, O Lord that your faithfulness will continue throughout all generations, in Jesus name!

We declare, O Lord that you will keep us from harm; you will watch over our lives; you will watch over our coming and our going both now and for evermore, in Jesus name! **(Psalms. 121)**

Thank you O Lord for the assurance that you are watching over us even when we sleep, in Jesus name! **(Psalms. 13:5-6)**

We declare, O Lord that you will drive those that do evil away from us and that you will protect us from their influence, in Jesus name! **(Ps. 66:1-4)**

We will shout with joy to you O Lord, we will sing the glory of your name and make your praise glorious. How awesome are your deeds! So great is your power that your enemies cringe before you, in Jesus name!

We declare, O Lord that that we will give you thanks for you answered us, in Jesus name! **(Psalms. 118:21)**

"Finally, brethren, whatsoever things are true, whatsoever things are honest, whatsoever things are just, whatsoever things are pure, whatsoever things are lovely, whatsoever things are of good report; if there be any virtue, and if there be any praise, think on these things."

Phil4:8

CHAPTER 1
The Spirit of Persistence

"For a just man falleth seven times, and riseth up again: but the wicked shall fall into mischief." **Proverb 24:16**

The Spirit of Persistence is the most admirable Spirits any believer will ever desire to possess. It is the determination to become successful over any particular trade, business, and academic, and employment, etc. regardless of the prevailing challenges, oppositions, failure, or setbacks.

The Spirit of Persistence is that *spirit* in us that will never give up the desire to try again, or go on one more time. It is that *Spirit* in us, that makes us fight to the finish, thrive to succeed, lunch a desperate comeback, in the face of great adversity, and tribulation.

It is written, *"For a just man falleth seven times, and riseth up again: but the wicked shall fall into mischief."*

I love to say that those who give up on their dreams, and vision in life will never become successful. *For unless we prevail and do not give up in life we will never prevail or succeed in life.* The point I am try to make is that, *the Spirit of Persistence* is the master skill for anyone who desire to succeed in their life time.

For most of us, the idea of failure, and hardship is unbearable, No one want to be associated with failure, opposition, or hardship in life. That is why we must all strive to develop the Spirit of Persistence in life.

Often the only difference between those who succeed and those who fail is The Spirit of Persistence.

It's relatively easy to persist when things are going well and in the direction we desire it to flow. But it is a different situation when we suffer failure, setbacks, and opposition, especially in the things that we are passionate about in life.

Chapter 1 - The Spirit of Persistence

The Characteristics of Persistent People

1. BURNING VISION

It is written, *"Where there is no vision, the people perish: but he that keepeth the law, happy is he."* **Proverb29:18**

Persistent people are men and women whose vision, and goal drives and motivates them to succeed in life despite opposition, setbacks, and obstacles. They are often visionaries who believe they were born for a greater purpose in life, bigger than simply earning a living. Their vision is deeply ingrained, and they focus on it constantly with great emotion, and energy. This vision usually, drives them with a purpose their entire life span.

2. A BURNING DESIRE

It is written, *"Therefore I say unto you, What things soever ye desire, when ye pray, believe that ye receive them, and ye shall have them."* **Mark11:24**

Entrepreneur and motivational speaker Jim Rohn once said, *"If you really want to do something, you'll find a way. If you don't, you'll find an excuse."*

For the most part, most persistent people have a burning desire driven with a passion to succeed in life, despite any prevailing obstacle.

They do not accept excuses, rather, they look for a way out. I love to believe that their burning desire and passion to succeed is what produces the Spirit of Persistence in them. They are not deterred by rejection, repeated failures, nor dead ends. Rather, they persist until a major breakthroughs is recorded. Persistent people have what I call inner strength that keep them focus in the face of adversity.

3. INNER CONFIDENCE

It is written *"And this is the confidence that we have in him, that, if we ask any thing according to his will, he heareth us."* **1John5:14**.

Chapter 1 - The Spirit of Persistence

Most people who overcame hardship and prevailing challenges are men and women of inner confidence.

The word of God says *"Confidence in an unfaithful man in time of trouble is like a broken tooth, and a foot out of joint." For unless you have inner confidence, everything will discourage you in life."*

4. THEY TRUST IN THE LORD

In my opinion highly persistent people are men and women who trust in the Lord. It is written *"They that trust in the Lord shall be as mount Zion, which cannot be removed, but abideth for ever."* **Psalms 125:1**.

These are men and women of self-confidence. Everyone knows that it is very difficult to stay continually motivated, particularly during difficult times when there are no sign of progress.

Highly persistent people rely upon God, their self-confidence to continue down the path toward their eventual goals.

They are persuaded and motivated to thrive and achieve the desired outcome in due time. It is written *" For the vision is yet for an appointed time, but at the end it shall speak, and not lie: though it tarry, wait for it; because it will surely come, it will not tarry."* **Hab2:3**

They believe the results of the efforts they make today may not be seen for a long time, but they strongly believe that everything they do will count toward their outcome in the end.

5. ABILITY TO ADJUST AND ADAPT

Highly Persistent people have the greatest ability to adjust and adapt to various action plan, short time goal, and orientation plan. They do not stubbornly persist in the face of a dead end when their plan is not working, but rather they look for better ways to achieve their desired outcome.

Highly Persistent people see their journey as a series of dead ends, detours, and adjustments, but have faith in God to make it in the end.

Chapter 1 - The Spirit of Persistence

They are not tied into their ego and are quickly willing to admit when something is not working. Also they are quick to adapt to the ideas of others that have been proven productive.

6. THEY EMBRACE OBSTACLES AS OPPORTUNITIES

Highly Persistent people realize that any goal worth reaching will take time, effort, and continuously learning new patterns. They always embrace threats and obstacles as opportunities.

One of my mentors answered a journalist who asked Him if he ever had failure, setbacks, and obstacles in life? He said and I quote, *"May be it came and I did not know."*

Highly Persistent people are open to new ideas, willing to face challenges and continue looking for ways to incorporate these into the desired outcome

ROLE MODELS THAT ACT AS GUIDES AND MENTORS

Although it may seem that highly persistent people act alone and don't need anyone, most of them have designated mentors who the follow, admire and emulate. These are mentors who have deeply impacted their lives. You will know who these people are since persistent people will often quote them. Persistent people usually stand out from their environment and are often misun-derstood or ridiculed because they can make those around them feel uncomfortable.

Having strongly ingrained models helps persistent people sustain and motivate themselves in an environment that is not always supportive.

The primary component for anyone of us to succeed in life is the spirit of persistence. This Spirit of persistence is the power of perseverance, the never giving up mentality, even in the face of trial and tribulation. Jesus said, *"Have faith in God"* **Mark11:22**.

Chapter 1 - The Spirit of Persistence

Everyone with a Persistent spirit is a winner for life. The truth is those who achieve great things in life, are those who do not quit, in the assignment God has called them to do.

"Weeping may endure for a night, but joy cometh in the morning." **Psalms30:5**

For anyone of us to succeed in life, we must learn to resist the devil, never accept failure as the final resolve, but never give up in the things God has called us to do in life.

"For to him that is joined to all the living there is hope: for a living dog is better than a dead lion." **Eccl9:4**

"And one of the elders saith unto me, Weep not: behold, the Lion of the tribe of Judah, the Root of David, hath prevailed to open the book, and to loose the seven seals thereof." **Rev 5:5**

No great achievement is possible without persistent work – **Bertrand Russell**

A distinguishing attributes of those who succeed in life against those who don't is the Spirit of Persistence.

So many folks have the capacity to set goals, and plan toward success, yet only hand few succeed, why? The truth is only a few of us persist in life to achieve the desired outcome.

"The most interesting thing about a postage stamp is the persistence with which it sticks to its job." – **Napoleon Hill**

The Spirit of Persistence is the master skill to all round-success in life. It is easier to relax and do nothing, or just live in our comfort zone, rather than face the uncertainty and discomfort of sailing through our goals.

But if you want to create change in your life and achieve great success in life, now is the time to develop the Spirit of Persistence inside of your heart.

Chapter 1 - The Spirit of Persistence

Ways to develop Persistence Spirit:

1. Recognize Your Heart Desires

"Delight thyself also in the Lord: and he shall give thee the desires of thine heart." **Psalms37:4**

I believe before anyone can develop the Spirit of Persistence and eventually achieve success, we need to first identify our heart desire. We can do this by simply asking God in prayer.

We are told *"Ask, and it shall be given you; seek, and ye shall find; knock, and it shall be opened unto you: For every one that asketh receiveth; and he that seeketh findeth; and to him that knocketh it shall be opened."* **Mathew7:7-8**

2. Keep a Positive Attitude

It is written *"For as he thinketh in his heart, so is he: Eat and drink, saith he to thee; but his heart is not with thee."* **Proverb23:7**.

For unless we think right, we will never act right. A positive attitude is vital for the Spirit of persistent to thrive, and motivate us. A positive attitude will keep us inspired, despite short-coming, and setbacks.

3. Develop A Winning Spirit

"Let this mind be in you, which was also in Christ Jesus: Who, being in the form of God, thought it not robbery to be equal with God:" **Phil2:5-6**.

If anyone of us must succeed in life we must carry a winning Spirit. It is written *"For whatsoever is born of God overcometh the world: and this is the victory that overcometh the world, even our faith"* **1John5:4**.

Jesus persevered to the cross, most persistent people are men and women of patience and endurance.

"For who hath known the mind of the Lord, that he may instruct him? but we have the mind of Christ." **1cor2:16**.

Chapter 1 - The Spirit of Persistence

The Spirit of Persistence means more than endurance, or long suffering in life. The bible says *"he that endured to the end shall be saved."*

If I may say this, the life and well-being of the believer is in the hands of God like a bow and arrow in the hands of an archer. The truth is, no matter what the enemy will throw at us, we are more than conqueror through Christ.

It is written *"Nay, in all these things we are more than conquerors through him that loved us."* **Romans8:37**

"What shall we then say to these things? If God be for us, who can be against us?" **Romans8:31**

"Ye are of God, little children, and have overcome them: because greater is he that is in you, than he that is in the world." **1John4:4**

"For whatsoever is born of God overcometh the world: and this is the victory that overcometh the world, even our faith." **1John5:4**

"And he said unto them, Ye are from beneath; I am from above: ye are of this world; I am not of this world." **John 8:23**

"And he answered, Fear not: for they that be with us are more than they that be with them." **2 King 6:16**

"He that cometh from above is above all: he that is of the earth is earthly, and speaketh of the earth: he that cometh from heaven is above all." **John 3:31**

"And hath raised us up together, and made us sit together in heavenly places in Christ Jesus." **Ephesians 2:6**

How do I Resist the devil?

1. *"Submit yourselves therefore to God. Resist the devil, and he will flee from you."* **James 4:7**

"Whatever you do not want in life, we must never watch nor tolerate them." For unless we resist the devil, he will not flea away from us.

Chapter 1 - The Spirit of Persistence

It is written *"Know ye not, that to whom ye yield yourselves servants to obey, his servants ye are to whom ye obey; whether of sin unto death, or of obedience unto righteousness?"* **Romans 6:16**

2. *"Neither be ye sorry; for the joy of the Lord is your strength."* **Neh8:10**

It is easy to make up excuses, and complain in life. For unless we make the joy of the Lord our strength, we will not be able to resist the devil. We were told *"Be sober, be vigilant; because your adversary the devil, as a roaring lion, walketh about, seeking whom he may devour:"* **1 Peter5:8**.

As long as you complain in life, you will always attract the devil into your life. Hear this, *"Neither murmur ye, as some of them also murmured, and were destroyed of the destroyer."* **1cor10:10**

3. *"For this is the will of God, even your sanctification, that ye should abstain from fornication:"* **1theo4:3**

If we must resist the devil we must stay away from sin. A life of sin is a life of wickedness. A life of sin is a life against the will and ordinances of God. Do you want to serve God? Then flea from sin.

"Now we know that God heareth not sinners: but if any man be a worshipper of God, and doeth his will, him he heareth." **John9:31**.

I love for you to hear this *"Behold, the Lord's hand is not shortened, that it cannot save; neither his ear heavy that it cannot hear: But your iniquities have separated between you and your God, and your sins have hid his face from you, that he will not hear."* **Isaia59:1-2**

What are we saying?

The devil has been defeated over two thousand years ago. Just about anyone of us can do great things for the kingdom of God. I like for you to remain inspired, you will succeed in the midst of challenges. Most of the things we call obstacles are opportunities in disguise.

Chapter 1 - The Spirit of Persistence

I pray God grant you revelation and understanding to dominate and rule your world in Jesus Mighty Name.

I love to say that the answer to a man's prayer is an idea of what to do in life. There is a divine vision for you. I pray you encounter and discover it in your life time.

Whatever God is calling us to do, we must look for people who have done it in time past. It is written *"The thing that hath been, it is that which shall be; and that which is done is that which shall be done: and there is no new thing under the sun."* **Ecl1:9**

What I am saying is for everyone to be persistent in our effort and desire to succeed in life. We must, therefore, develop purpose, a goal, and a vision for our life and family. We must always believe in God. I love to tell you that there is a way up, a way forward, and a way out of any prevailing predicament you may find your self.

I can only encourage your life through the pages of this small book.

It is written, *"Whatsoever thy hand findeth to do, do it with thy might; for there is no work, nor device, nor knowledge, nor wisdom, in the grave, whither thou goest."* **Eccl9:10**

"For even when we were with you, this we commanded you, that if any would not work, neither should he eat." **2theo3:10**

"The sluggard will not plow by reason of the cold; therefore shall he beg in harvest, and have nothing." **Proverb20:4**

"He also that is slothful in his work is brother to him that is a great waster." **Proverb18:9**

"The soul of the sluggard desireth, and hath nothing: but the soul of the diligent shall be made fat." **Proverb13:4**

"He becometh poor that dealeth with a slack hand: but the hand of the diligent maketh rich." **Proverb10:4**

Chapter 1 - The Spirit of Persistence

Jeremiah 29:11

" For I know the plans I have for you," declares the LORD, "plans to prosper you and not to harm you, plans to give you hope and a future."

Psalm 27:4

"One thing I ask from the LORD, this only do I seek: that I may dwell in the house of the LORD all the days of my life, to gaze on the beauty of the LORD and to seek him in his temple."

Psalm 34:8

"Taste and see that the LORD is good; blessed is the one who takes refuge in him."

Proverbs 17:17

"A friend loves at all times, and a brother is born for a time of adversity."

John 15:13

"Greater love has no one than this: to lay down one's life for one's friends."

Romans 8:28

"And we know that in all things God works for the good of those who love him, who have been called according to his purpose."

Romans 8:31

"What, then, shall we say in response to these things? If God is for us, who can be against us?"

Romans 15:13

"May the God of hope fill you with all joy and peace as you trust in him, so that you may overflow with hope by the power of the Holy Spirit."

Chapter 1 - The Spirit of Persistence

Romans 8:38-39

"For I am convinced that neither death nor life, neither angels nor demons, neither the present nor the future, nor any powers, neither height nor depth, nor anything else in all creation, will be able to separate us from the love of God that is in Christ Jesus our Lord."

1 Corinthians 13:12

"For now we see only a reflection as in a mirror; then we shall see face to face. Now I know in part; then I shall know fully, even as I am fully known."

Lamentations 3:22-23

"Because of the LORD's great love we are not consumed, for his compassions never fail. They are new every morning; great is your faithfulness."

2 Corinthians 4:16-18

"Therefore we do not lose heart. Though outwardly we are wasting away, yet inwardly we are being renewed day by day. 17 For our light and momentary troubles are achieving for us an eternal glory that far outweighs them all. So we fix our eyes not on what is seen, but on what is unseen, since what is seen is temporary, but what is unseen is eternal."

1 Corinthians 16:13

"Be on your guard; stand firm in the faith; be courageous; be strong."

CHAPTER 2
The Benefits of Persistence

"And ye shall be hated of all men for my name's sake: but he that shall endure unto the end, the same shall be saved." **Mark 13:13**

In my opinion we must all be persistent and consistent with our prayer life, worship, tithes, and offering unto God. None of us will be able to make it into the kingdom of God without the Spirit of persistence. Usually things don't usually go as planned.

It is written *"There are many devices in a man's heart; nevertheless the counsel of the Lord, that shall stand."* **Proverb 19:21**

"Declaring the end from the beginning, and from ancient times the things that are not yet done, saying, My counsel shall stand, and I will do all my pleasure:" **Isaiah 46:10**

Chapter 2 - The Benefits of Persistence

We must all be ready to confront opposition, and deal with inevitable dead end, rejection, failure, and roadblocks against our desired future.

"These things I have spoken unto you, that in me ye might have peace. In the world ye shall have tribulation: but be of good cheer; I have overcome the world." **John16:33**

"For a great door and effectual is opened unto me, and there are many adversaries." **1cor16:9**

"For our light affliction, which is but for a moment, worketh for us a far more exceeding and eternal weight of glory;" **2cor4:17**

For anyone to be dynamic and adapt to personal or external forces against their lives, they must be driven with a sense of purpose in life. Mere planning doesn't identify uncertainties in life. It is *the Spirit of Persistence* and tenacity that enhances success.

Rev Dr. Martin Luther King Jr. when he said, and I quote *"If you can't fly you run, if you can't run you walk, if you can't walk you crawl. But no matter what, you keep moving forward."*

"For which of you, intending to build a tower, sitteth not down first, and counteth the cost, whether he have sufficient to finish it?" **Luke14:28**

Persistence increases our prayer life

It is inevitable to for anyone to genuinely pray to God, often and persist without any substantial change in their life. In my opinion, persistent in prayer increase the hunger and fire to pray unto God the more.

Persistence increases faith in our heart

For those of us that have been praying consistently and persisted without stopping, you guys know that as long as you persist in prayers, faith in God increases.

Chapter 2 - The Benefits of Persistence

Persistence gives us hope

The Spirit of Persistent grants everyone courage, hope, and faith.

Hindrances of the Spirit of Persistence

--Doubt--

Doubter never settle with one job, they run from one trade to the other. You must settle with what God has called you to do in life. For unless you believe in your own abilities and in God, you will not succeed in the face of challenges. As a believer, we have no reason to doubt the word of God, or the revelations you received from the Lord. Unless the Lord has not spoken to you.

"Who is he that saith, and it cometh to pass, when the Lord commandeth it not?" **Lamentation3:37**

It is written, *"A double minded man is unstable in all his ways."* **James1:8**

--Unbelief--

You only live once, therefore make the most out of life. There is no reason for anyone to suffer from unbelief in life. We are commanded to believe God and to believe God's prophet in life. It is written *"....Believe in the Lord your God, so shall ye be established; believe his prophets, so shall ye prosper."* **2chronicle20:20**

One man said without a mentor, you are left in the hand of the tormentor. Talking about Jesus the bible says *" And he could there do no mighty work, save that he laid his hands upon a few sick folk, and healed them. And he marvelled because of their unbelief. And he went round about the villages, teaching."* **Mark6:5-6**.

--- Fear--

"There were they in great fear, where no fear was: for God hath scattered the bones of him that encampeth against thee: thou hast put them to shame, because God hath despised them" **Psalms53:5**

Chapter 2 - The Benefits of Persistence

What are you afraid of, there is no harm in trial. Fear of the unknown will deter anyone from taking a bold step concerning your future in life.

Apostle Paul said *"For a great door and effectual is opened unto me, and there are many adversaries."* **1cor16:9**

---Sin--

"Behold, the Lord's hand is not shortened, that it cannot save; neither his ear heavy that it cannot hear: But your iniquities have separated between you and your God, and your sins have hid his face from you, that he will not hear." **Isaiah59:1-2**

"For sin shall not have dominion over you: for ye are not under the law, but under grace." **Romans6:14**

"If I regard iniquity in my heart, the Lord will not hear me." **Psalms66:18**

"Thy word have I hid in mine heart, that I might not sin against thee." **Psalms119:11**.

Every time you are doing anything contrary to the will of God. Any action that contradicts the Holy Scripture and the commandment of the Lord. If you must succeed in life you must live right. If we must share our testimonies with others, we must do it scripturally.

"The soul that sinneth, it shall die. The son shall not bear the iniquity of the father, neither shall the father bear the iniquity of the son: the righteousness of the righteous shall be upon him, and the wickedness of the wicked shall be upon him." **Ezekiel18:20**

WE MUST REPENT OF OUR SINS

Wherefore seeing we also are compassed about with so great a cloud of witnesses, let us lay aside every weight, and the sin which doth so easily beset us, and let us run with patience the race that is set before us, **Hebrew12:1**.

We must not allow sin to destroy our calling and destiny in life. We must therefore repent of any known sin in our lives before God can restore our destiny.

Chapter 2 - The Benefits of Persistence

"For sin shall not have dominion over you: for ye are not under the law, but under grace." **Romans6:14**

Every time we yield to sin, we place ourselves in captivity. We must all strive to forsake sin and do away with every evil that dent our Christian dignity. Know ye not, that to whom ye yield yourselves servants to obey, his servants ye are to whom ye obey; whether of sin unto death, or of obedience unto righteousness? **Romans6:16**

It is written, *"Be not overcome of evil, but overcome evil with good."* **Romans12:21**.

We must all repent of any know sin that dents our Christian walk with the Lord Jesus Christ.

Apostle Paul had this to say….

"I find then a law, that, when I would do good, evil is present with me. For I delight in the law of God after the inward man: But I see another law in my members, warring against the law of my mind,

and bringing me into captivity to the law of sin which is in my members. O wretched man that I am! who shall deliver me from the body of this death? I thank God through Jesus Christ our Lord. So then with the mind I myself serve the law of God; but with the flesh the law of sin." **Romans 7:21-25.**

The above scripture makes a lot of sin if you examine your own life. Evil is present every time we strive to do good. What shall we say then? Shall we continue in sin, that grace may abound? God forbid. How shall we, that are dead to sin, live any longer therein? **Romans 6:1-2.**

"Examine yourselves, whether ye be in the faith; prove your own selves. Know ye not your own selves, how that Jesus Christ is in you, except ye be reprobates?" **2cor 13:5**

Although most faith people live in denial about the work of the flesh, from my own scriptural understanding everyone operating within the scope of **Galatians 5:20-21** is classified as a sinner.

Chapter 2 - The Benefits of Persistence

How to I come out of sin?

Although we are all sinners, it takes a will power of the mind for us to repent and come out of sin. So many people have died because they could not let go the sin that easily best them go. Someone who The Lord Jesus delivered from drug addiction, overdosed on drugs and died.

A great man of God who repented because of alcohol in the family died of excessive alcohol abuse. We must make up our mind for good if we must come out of sin. We must confess, and forsake it in the mighty name of Jesus.

The word says as many as received him, to them gave He power to become the sons of God. Even to them that believe on his name.

To qualify for divine visitation do the following sincerely;

1) Acknowledge that you are a sinner and that He died for you. **Rom3:23**.

2) Repent of your sins. **Acts 3:19, Luke13:5, 2Peter3:9**

3) Believe in your heart that Jesus died for your sin. **Romans10:10**

4) Confess Jesus as the Lord over your life. **Romans10:10, Acts2:21**

Now repeat this Prayer after me

Say Lord Jesus, I accept you today, as my Lord and my savior, forgive me of my sins wash me with your blood. Right now, I believe, I am sanctified, I am save, I am free, I am free from the Power of sin to serve the Lord Jesus. Thank you Lord for saving me. Amen.

Chapter 2 - The Benefits of Persistence

CONCLUSION

"For a just man falleth seven times, and riseth up again: but the wicked shall fall into mischief." **Proverb 24:16**

And said to his servant, Go up now, look toward the sea. And he went up, and looked, and said, There is nothing. And he said, Go again seven times." **1 King 18:43**

My purpose of writing this book is defeated if you finish reading this material and still did not confess Jesus Christ as your personal Lord and savior.

"Therefore if any man be in Christ, he is a new creature: old things are passed away; behold, all things are become new." **2cor 5:17**

Now repeat this Prayer after me;

Say Lord Jesus, I accept you today, as my Lord and my savior, forgive me of my sins wash me with your blood. Right now, I believe, I am sanctified, I am save, I am free, I am free from the Power of sin to serve the Lord Jesus. Thank you Lord for saving me. Amen.

Are you a sinner or a born again believer?

What must I do to determine my divine visitation?

To determine divine visitation you must be born again. The word says as many as received him, to them gave He power to become the sons of God. Even to them that believe on his name.

To qualify for divine visitation do the following sincerely;

1) Acknowledge that you are a sinner and that He died for you. **Rom3:23**.

2) Repent of your sins. **Acts 3:19, Luke13:5, 2Peter3:9**

3) Believe in your heart that Jesus died for your sin. **Romans10:10**

4) Confess Jesus as the Lord over your life. **Romans10:10, Acts2:21**

Chapter 2 - The Benefits of Persistence

Now repeat this Prayer after me

Say Lord Jesus, I accept you today, as my Lord and my savior, forgive me of my sins wash me with your blood. Right now, I believe, I am sanctified, I am save, I am free, I am free from the Power of sin to serve the Lord Jesus. Thank you Lord for saving me. Amen.

Congratulations: YOU ARE NOW A BORN AGAIN CHRISTAIN

I adjure you to watch the Spirit of God bear witness with your Spirit confirming His word with signs following. The word says The Spirit itself beareth witness with our spirit, that we are the children of God. Join a bible believing church or join us on our weekly and Sunday worship services at 343 Sanford Avenue Newark New Jersey 07106.

WISDOM KEYS

Every Productive Society is a society heading to the top

Millions of Nigerians run away from Nigeria, very few Nigerians stay in Nigeria.

My decision to return Nigeria is the will of God for my life

My short coming in America after 18 years, trained me to be wise, to think, reflect and reason appropriately.

If you train your mind to reason it will train your hands to earn money.

It is absurd to use the money of the heathen to build the kingdom of the living God.

Every Ministry reveals its agenda and goal either at the beginning or at the end. Be careful of your life it is your first Ministry.

The average American mind is conditioned for a continual quest to get new things and (discard the former) and throw away old things.

Chapter 2 - The Benefits of Persistence

When I considered well, my BMW jeep became my initial deposit for the work of the ministry in Nigeria

Everyone is waiting for you to change your mind until you change your thinking nothing changes around you.

Multiple academic degrees in other discipline gave me the chance to think, reflect and reason

What so everyone are thinking and reflecting at the moment reveals you to the time and the now factor

All events and intents are the product of precise thought processes, accurate reason every event is designed for a designated timeline

Wisdom is your ability to think, to create and invent. If you can think wise enough you will come out of penury

The distance between you and success is your creative ability to think reason and reflect accurate.

Success is the result of hard work, commitment resolve and determination learning from past mistakes and failing.

If you organize your mind you have organized your life and destiny.

There is a thin line between success and failure. If you look above and beyond you are on your way to success.

Wealth is your ability to think, power is your ability to reason and success is your ability to be informed.

If you can make use of your mind by thinking and reasoning God will make use of your life and destiny.

Think and Be Great

Reflect, Reason, think and be great

Famous people are born of woman

Chapter 2 - The Benefits of Persistence

That you will make it is your intention; that you will survive is your resolve, that you will succeed with changes is your determination, personal efforts and hard work.

No man was born a failure. Lack of vision is the end product of failure.

Working with mental patients encourages and aspire me to be a productive observant and dedicated to my assignment.

Successful people are not magicians, it is the will power combined with hard work, and determination and a resolve to succeed that make them succeed.

In the unequivocal state of the mind, intention is not a location or a position it is the state of the mind.

So many people think that they think. The mind is used to think reflect and reason. You will remain blind with your eye open until you can see with your mind by thinking.

There is no favoritism in accurate and precise calculation

The Power of Persistance by Franklin N. Abazie

Although knowledge is power, information is the key and gateway to a great future.

It will take the hand of God to move the hand of man.

With the backing of the great wise God, nothing will disconnect you from your inheritance.

As long as you have wisdom and understanding of God, Satan and evil cannot manipulate your life and destiny.

You have come this far by yourself judgment and decision you have made in the past, now lean and listen to God for another dimension of greatness.

Great people are common people it is extra ordinary effort and the price of sacrifice that produces greatness.

As a mental direct care worker I saw a great pastor and a motivational speaker within myself.

Menial job does not reduce your self-worth, until you resolve to achieve greatness see greatness in all you do; you will never count in your community

Chapter 2 - The Benefits of Persistence

The principle of Jesus will solve your gambling and addiction problems

The man of Jesus will lead you into heaven,

Everyone have their self-appraisal and what they think about you. Until you discover yourself other opinion about you will alter the real you.

Supervisors and directors are just a position in the chain of command in a work place. Never allow your supervisor hierarchy to alter your opinion about yourself.

Everyone can come out of debt if they make up their mind.

That I am not a decision maker at work does not diminish my contribution to my world.

Although it appears like it was a poor decision to accept a direct care employment at a psychiatric hospital as I reflect of my nine years of experience, it became apparent that I have learnt and experienced enough for my next assignment.

Self-encouragement and determination is a resolve of the heart.

The Power of Persistance by Franklin N. Abazie

If you are determined to make a difference, and do the things that make a difference you will eventually make a difference.

Good things do not come easy

Short cuts will cut your life short.

Those who look ahead move ahead.

Life is all about making an impact. In your life time strive to make an impact in your community.

Make friends and connect with people who are moving ahead of you in life.

If you can look around well you have come a long way in your life, made a lot of difference and realized a lot of success in life.

If you are my old friend, hurry up to reach out to me before I become a stranger to you.

Everything I am blessed with inspirations from God, that change my definition and interpretation of the world around me.

I thought I was stagnant and lonely until I looked around and noticed my children running around and my wife cooking.

Chapter 2 - The Benefits of Persistence

At 40 I resigned my Job to seek the Lord forever.

My ministry took a drastic rise to the top when the wisdom of God visited me with knowledge and understanding.

You will be a better person if you understand the characteristics of your personality – your mood swings attitudes and habits.

It is the seed of love you sow into the heart of a child and a woman that you reap in due time.

Love is not selfish, love share everything including the concealed secrets of the mind.

As long as you have a prayer life and a bible; you will never feel lonely, rejected and idle in the race of life.

When good friends disconnect from you, let them go, they might have seen something new in a different direction.

Confidence in yourself and in God is the only way to bring you out of captivity

Never train a child to waste his/her time.

The mind is the greatest assets of a great future.

The Power of Persistance by Franklin N. Abazie

You walk by common sense run by principles and fly by instruction.

Those who fly in flight of life fly alone.

Up in the air you are alone. No one can toll you accept the compass of knowledge and information

I have seen a tolling vehicle I have seen a tolling ship I have never seen a tolling airplane.

I exercise my judgment and make a decision every minute of the day.

Decisions are crucial, critical and vital with reference to your future.

So many people wish for a great future. You can only work towards a great future.

Your celebrity status began when you discovered your talent. What are you good at? Work at it with all commitment.

Prayers will sustain you but the wisdom of God will prosper you.

When I met Oyedepo, his teachings changed my perspective, but when I met Ibiyeomie; His teaching changed my perception.

Chapter 2 - The Benefits of Persistence

I will be successful in ministry if only I concentrate and focus my energy in the work of the ministry.

It took the late Dr. Vincent Pearle Norman's book to open my mind towards kingdom success.

CHAPTER 3

PRAYER OF SALVATION

"Neither is there salvation in any other: for there is none other name under heaven given among men, whereby we must be saved." **Acts 4:12.**

The purpose of this small book will be defeated if you finish reading without hearing a message about your salvation. Hear me out! Your sanctification, and Salvation is very important to God, and to your soul.

Are you saved?

To be saved we must be born again!

The word says as many as received him, to them gave He power to become the sons of God. Even to them that believe on his name.

Chapter 3 - Prayer of Salvation

To qualify for divine visitation do the following sincerely,

1) Acknowledge that you are a sinner and that He died for you. **Rom3:23.**

2) Repent of your sins. **Acts 3:19, Luke13:5, 2Peter3:9**

3) Believe in your heart that Jesus died for your sin. **Romans10:10**

4) Confess Jesus as the Lord over your life. **Romans10:10, Acts2:21**

Now repeat this Prayer after me

Say Lord Jesus, I accept you today, as my Lord and my savior, forgive me of my sins wash me with your blood. Right now, I believe, I am sanctified, I am save, I am free, I am free from the Power of sin to serve the Lord Jesus. Thank you Lord for saving me. Amen.

Congratulations:

YOU ARE NOW A BORN AGAIN CHRISTIAN

I adjure you to watch the Spirit of God bear witness with your Spirit confirming His word with signs following. The word says The Spirit itself beareth witness with our spirit, that we are the children of God.

MIRACLE CARE OUTREACH

"...But that the members should have the same care one for another" **1cor12:25**

We are all members of the body of Christ. Jesus commanded us to love our neighbor as ourselves. This includes caring for one another as a member of one body. True love is expressed in caring and giving. The word says for God so Love He gave….

Reach out to someone in need of Jesus, help someone in crisis find Christ. Look out and prove your love to Jesus by caring and inviting your friends and associates to find Jesus the Healer.

Chapter 3 - Prayer of Salvation

Invite your friends to our Home Care Cell Fellowship (Miracle chapel Intl Satellite fellowship) In the USA at 33 Schley Street Newark New Jersey 07112.

If you are in Nigeria—**MIRACLE OF GOD MINISTRIES**

A.K.A "MIRACLE CHAPEL INTL"
Mpama –Egbu-Owerri Imo state Nigeria.

(Home Care Cell fellowship Group). We meet every Tuesday at 6:00pm-7:00pm.

LIFE IS NOT ALL ABOUT DURATION BUT ITS ALL ABOUT DONATION

What does the above statement mean?....

"Life consists not in accumulation of material wealth.." **Luke12:15.**

"But it's all about liberality....meaning-what you can give and share with others." **Proverb11:25.**

When you live for others--You live forever-because you out live your generation by the legacy you live behind after you depart into glory to be with the Lord. But when you live to yourself - you are reduced to self—you are easily forgotten when you die and depart in glory.

Permit me to admonish you today to live your life to be a blessing to a soul connected to you today.

I want you to know that so many souls are connected and looking up to you, and through you so many souls will be saved and rescued from destruction. Will you disciple someone today to find Jesus Christ?

"As a genuine Christian; it is your duty to evangelize Jesus Christ to all you meet on your way. Jesus is still in the healing business-Jesus is still doing miracles from time of old to now.

Therefore tell someone about Jesus Christ today, disciple and bring them to Church."

John 1:45 Philip findeth Nathanael….

Chapter 3 - Prayer of Salvation

Please to prove the sincerity of your love for God today; please become a soul winner. The dignity of your Christianity is hidden in your boldness to proclaim and evangelize Jesus Christ to all you meet on your way.

There is a question mark on the integrity of your Christianity until you become a life soul winner. Invite someone to join us worship the Lord Jesus this coming Sunday.

MIRACLE OF GOD MINISTRIES

PILLARS OF THE COMMISSION

We Believe, Preach and Practice the following,

1) We believe and preach Salvation to every living human being

2) We believe and preach Repentance and forgiveness of sins

3) We believe and preach the baptism of the Holy Spirit and Spiritual gifts

4) We believe and teach the Prosperity

5) We believe and preach Divine Healing and Miracles (Signs &Wonder)

6) We believe and preach Faith

7) We believe and Proclaim the Power of God (Supernatural)

8) We believe and Proclaim Praise& Worship to God

Chapter 3 - Prayer of Salvation

9) We believe and preach Wisdom

10) We believe and preach Holiness (Consecration)

11) We believe and preach Vision

12) We believe and teach the Word of God

13) We believe and teach Success

14) We believe and practice Prayer

15) We believe and teach Deliverance

This 15 stones form the Pillars of Our Commission.

Become part of this church family and follow this great move of God.

MY HEART FELT PRAYER FOR YOU

As long as you persist in prayers, God will fight for you. I see you succeeding in your life. I like to encourage you with a word of prayer. It is written Therefore, my beloved brethren, be ye steadfast, unmovable, always abounding in the work of the Lord, forasmuch as ye know that your labor is not in vain in the Lord.

Now let me Pray for you:

Lord Jesus, I thank you for life and for all your provisions upon our lives, thus far. Father reach out to this precious love one and show us your glory. I thank You for what You have done. But I praise You for what You will do for us even now. In Jesus Mighty Name. **Amen**

CHAPTER 4
ABOUT THE AUTHOR

Rev Franklin N Abazie is the founding and Presiding Pastor of Miracle of God Ministries with headquarters in Newark, New Jersey USA and a branch church in Owerri- Imo State Nigeria. He is following the footsteps of one of his mentors, Oral Roberts (Healing Evangelist) of the blessed memory.

The Lord passed Oral Roberts healing mantle two days before he went to be with the Lord at age 91 into the hand of healing evangelist-Rev Franklin N Abazie in a vision.

In all his services the Power and Presence of God is present to heal all in his audience. He is an ordained man of God with a Healing Ministry reviving the healing and miracle ministry of Jesus Christ of Nazareth.

Chapter 4 - About the Author

Pastor Franklin N Abazie, is called by God with a unique mandate:

"THE MOMENT IS DUE TO IMPACT YOUR WORLD THROUGH THE REVIVAL OF THE HEALING & MIRACLE MINISTRY OF JESUS CHRIST OF NAZARETH.

I AM SENDING YOU TO RESTORE HEALTH UNTO THEE AND I WILL HEAL THEE OF THY WOUNDS. SAID THE LORD OF HOST"

He is a gifted ardent Teacher of the word of God who operates also in the office of a Prophet, generating and attracting undeniable signs & wonders, special miracles and healings, with apostolic fireworks of the Holy Ghost.

He is the founding and presiding senior Pastor of this fast growing Healing ministry.

He has written over 86 inspirational, healing and transforming books covering almost all aspect of divine healing and life. He is happily married and blessed with children.

BOOKS BY REV FRANKLIN N ABAZIE

1) Commanding Abundance
2) The outcome of faith
3) Understanding the secret of prevailing prayers
4) Understanding the secret of the man God uses
5) Activating my due Season
6) Overcoming Divine Verdicts
7) The Outcome of Divine Wisdom
8) Understanding God's Restoration Mandate
9) Walking in the Victory and Authority of the truth
10) Gods Covenant Exemption
11) Destiny Restoration Pillars
12) Provoking Acceptable Praise
13) Understanding Divine Judgment
14) Activating Angelic Re-enforcement
15) Provoking Un-Merited Favor
16) The Benefits of the Speaking faith
17) Understanding Divine Arrangement

18) Understanding Divine Healing
19) The Mystery of Endurance
20) Obeying Divine Instructions
21) Understanding the Voice of God
22) Never give up on Hope
23) The prevailing Power of faith
24) Understanding Divine Prosperity
25) The Reward of Prayer
26) Covenant Keys to Answered Prayers
27) Activating the Forces of Vengeance
28) Put your faith to work
29) Where is your trust?
30) The Audacity of the Blood of Jesus
31) Redeeming Your Days
32) The force of Vision
33) Breaking the shackles of Family Curses
34) Wisdom for Marriage Stability
35) The winners Faith
36) The Prayer solution
37) The power of Prayer
38) The Effective Strategy of Prayer
39) The Prayer that Works
40) Walking in Forgiveness
41) ThePower of the Grace of God

42) The power of Persistence
43) Overcoming Divine verdicts
44) The audacity of the blood of Jesus.
45) The prevailing power of the blood of Jesus
46) The benefit of the speaking faith.
47) Fearless faith
48) Redeeming Your Days.
49) The Supernatural Power of Prophecy
50) The companionship of the Holy Spirit
51) Understanding Divine Judgement
52) Understanding Divine Prosperity
53) Dominating Controlling Forces
54) The winners Faith
55) Destiny Restoration Pillars
56) Developing Spiritual Muscles
57) Inexplicable faith
58) The lifestyle of Prayer
59) Developing a positive attitude in life.
60) The mystery of Divine supply
61) Encounter with God's Power
62) Walking in love
63) Praying in the Spirit
64) How to provoke your testimony

65) Walking in the reality of the Anointing
66) The reality of new birth
67) The price of freedom
68) The Supernatural power of faith
69) The Power of Persistence
70) The Intellectual Components of Redemption
71) Overcoming Fear
72) The Force of Vision
73) Overcoming Prevailing Challenges
74) The Power of the Grace of God
75) My life & Ministry
76) The Mystery of Praise

MIRACLE OF GOD MINISTRIES

NIGERIA CRUSADE 2012

MIRACLE OF GOD MINISTRIES
NIGERIA CRUSADE 2012

MIRACLE OF GOD MINISTRIES

NIGERIA CRUSADE

2012

MIRACLE OF GOD MINISTRIES

NIGERIA CRUSADE

2012

www.ingramcontent.com/pod-product-compliance
Lightning Source LLC
Chambersburg PA
CBHW021443080526
44588CB00009B/666